D1450181

Are VIDEO GAMES Too Violent?

By Nick Christopher

KidHaven
PUBLISHING

Published in 2018 by
KidHaven Publishing, an Imprint of Greenhaven Publishing, LLC
353 3rd Avenue
Suite 255
New York, NY 10010

Designer: Seth Hughes
Editor: Katie Kawa

Photo credits: Cover Stanislav Solntsev/DigitalVision/Getty Images; p. 5 (top) Kraig Scarbinsky/DigitalVision/Thinkstock; p. 5 (bottom) BSIP/UIG via Getty Images; p. 7 (game cover art) Game Shots/Alamy Stock Photo; p. 7 (game case) Barin Doru Cristian "thislooksgreat"; p. 7 (magnifying glass) sky_max/iStock/Thinkstock; p. 9 Asia Images Group/Shutterstock.com; p. 11 Alena Ozerova/Shutterstock.com; p. 13 (background) breakermaximus/Shutterstock.com; p. 13 (inset) Kreatiw/iStock/Thinkstock; p. 15 © iStockphoto.com/lovleah; p. 17 SerrNovik/iStock/Thinkstock; p. 19 © iStockphoto.com/FOTOKITA; p. 21 (notepad) ESB Professional/Shutterstock.com; p. 21 (markers) Kucher Serhii/Shutterstock.com; p. 21 (photo frame) FARBAI/iStock/Thinkstock; p. 21 (inset, left) monkeybusinessimages/iStock/Thinkstock; p. 21 (inset, middle-left) George Dolgikh/Shutterstock.com; p. 21 (inset, middle-right) MilicaStankovic/iStock/Thinkstock; p. 21 (inset, right) © iStockphoto.com/sezer66.

Cataloging-in-Publication Data

Names: Christopher, Nick.
Title: Are video games too violent? / Nick Christopher.
Description: New York : KidHaven Publishing, 2018. | Series: Points of view | Includes glossary and index.
Identifiers: ISBN 9781534524873 (pbk.) | 9781534524255 (library bound) | ISBN 9781534524880 (6 pack) | ISBN 9781534524262 (ebook)
Subjects: LCSH: Violence in video games–Juvenile literature. | Video games–Social aspects–Juvenile literature. | Video games–Psychological aspects–Juvenile literature. | Violence–Juvenile literature.
Classification: LCC GV1469.34.V56 C575 2018 | DDC 794.8–dc23

Printed in the United States of America

CPSIA compliance information: Batch #CW18KL: For further information contact Greenhaven Publishing LLC, New York, New York at 1-844-317-7404.

CONTENTS

The Video Game Debate   4

Rating Video Games   6

Making Informed Choices   8

Easy to Break the Rules   10

Are Video Games Helpful?   12

A Dangerous Connection   14

No Clear Link   16

Becoming Desensitized   18

Staying Open-Minded   20

Glossary   22

For More Information   23

Index   24

The Video Game
DEBATE

Do you like to play video games? If you do, you're not alone! Around 90 percent of children in the United States play video games. Many people think of video games as harmless fun, but some people worry that certain games are too **violent**.

This **debate** has been going on for many years, and people on both sides have strong opinions. Before you decide which side you agree with, it's helpful to know all the facts about video games and violence. This is called having an informed, or educated, opinion.

Know the Facts!

As of 2015, more than 85 percent of all video games had some amount of violence in them.

4

Video games can be fun to play, but they can also be very violent. Some people are afraid the violence in video games can make people act violently when they stop playing.

Rating
VIDEO GAMES

People have been playing video games at home since 1972, when the first home game system—the Magnavox Odyssey—was sold. Since then, video games have risen in popularity, and now most American homes have some kind of gaming system. Today, games can also be played on computers and smartphones.

Early video games didn't have the same amount of violence as some games have today. To help keep these violent video games out of children's hands, a ratings system was set up in 1994. These ratings show what ages should be playing certain games.

Know the Facts!

The rating system for video games also includes content descriptors, which describe parts of a game that might make it inappropriate for certain age groups. These include violence, blood, and use of drugs.

RATINGS CATEGORIES

rating	what it means
EARLY CHILDHOOD (**EC**)	The game is made for young children.
EVERYONE (**E**)	The game is appropriate for all ages.
EVERYONE 10+ (**E10+**)	The game is appropriate for everyone 10 years old and up.
TEEN (**T**)	The game is appropriate for players 13 years old and up.
MATURE (**M**)	The game is appropriate for players 17 years old and up.
ADULTS ONLY (**AO**)	The game is only for players 18 years old and up.

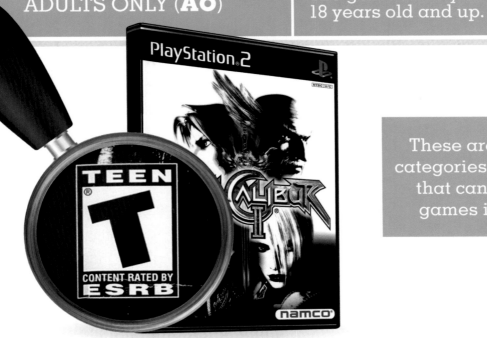

These are the main ratings categories, or kinds of ratings, that can be seen on video games in North America.

Making Informed
CHOICES

Video game ratings and content descriptors are supposed to help adults make decisions about the video games they buy for children. Also, stores aren't supposed to sell M-rated video games to anyone under 17 years old, and they're not supposed to sell AO-rated video games to anyone under 18 years old.

If these ratings are used properly, people are able to make informed choices about the games they play and the games they let children play. For example, a person can use the content descriptors to stay away from any video games that **contain** violence.

Know the Facts!

Video game ratings now also let players know if the game shares their location, allows them to **interact** with other people through the Internet, or asks them to spend money. These are called interactive elements.

Some adults play video games with their children. They believe learning as much as they can about the video games their children are playing can help protect their children from seeing too much violence.

THE RULES

Some people believe ratings keep video games from being too violent for the age group playing them. However, there are ways to get around the rules, and children can end up playing games many think are too violent.

The video game ratings system was created to make sure children were only playing games appropriate for their age group. That's not always how the system works, though. Kids can play games rated M and AO if an adult buys them. Also, even though stores aren't supposed to sell these games to people under the appropriate age, it's not illegal, so sometimes kids can still buy them.

Know the Facts!

The U.S. Supreme Court ruled in 2011 that no laws can be made to ban the sale of video games to anyone based on the violence in them.

Many popular video games are rated M. People younger than 17 often want to play them even if they're considered too violent for their age group.

Are Video Games HELPFUL?

If kids find a way to play violent video games, will this make them want to act violently? There are many different opinions on this issue. Some people believe playing violent video games could actually be a good thing for some people. These games may help people **channel** their **aggression** into a world that's not real.

One study showed that violent crime actually went down in the time around the **release** of certain video games. It's believed this may be because playing video games gives people something to do instead of acting out in violent ways.

Know the Facts!

A 2015 study showed that boys are more likely to play video games than girls. In the study, 84 percent of boys said they played video games, and 59 percent of girls said the same.

Some of the most popular video games are first-person shooter games, in which the player sees everything through the eyes of a shooter. Some people believe these games help people deal with aggression, while others think they cause more aggression.

ARMOR
100

AMMO
75

CONNECTION

Although some people believe violent video games might lower the amount of violence in the world, others strongly disagree. They think video games actually make people more aggressive. This was reported in a 2015 study by the American Psychological Association (APA), which is a group of scientists who study the way the human mind works.

Many scientists believe video games have too much violence in them and that the violence in them is too often **linked** with success. They believe video games put too much **focus** on killing, which teaches people to see hurting others as a way to win.

Know the Facts!

In July 2016, the American Academy of Pediatrics, which is a group of doctors who care for children, stated that playing violent video games was linked to more aggression in young people.

Some groups of scientists believe there is a strong connection between violent video games and anger and aggression in children. Aggressive children could hurt themselves or others.

15

LINK

Some studies show a link between video games and aggression, but what about video games and violent actions? Scientists still haven't found a clear link between playing violent video games and being more likely to **commit** acts of violence.

Some people have also found problems with studies linking aggression and violent video games. Children who are more aggressive may like to play violent video games, but that doesn't mean the games are causing them to be aggressive. Some scientists want to study this issue more before claiming video games are too violent.

Know the Facts!

In 2015, more than 230 **experts** came together to speak out against the APA's statements about video games and violence. These experts felt the APA was looking at video games in an outdated way.

16

Many people play video games that might be seen by some as too violent. However, most of these people don't commit acts of violence.

Becoming
DESENSITIZED

No direct link has been found yet between playing violent video games and acting violently, but that doesn't mean violent video games are harmless. Many video games show upsetting acts of violence. However, as people play the games more often and see these acts more often, the violence makes them less upset over time.

When people get used to violence, it's called becoming desensitized to it. People who are desensitized to acts of violence don't feel as upset about violent acts when they see them.

Know the Facts!

Empathy is the ability to understand and share another person's feelings. The APA found that playing violent video games led to a lower amount of empathy in the people they studied.

18

Leaders want to do whatever they can to stop mass shootings, or shootings in which many people are killed. Some believe banning violent video games is one way to do this because a number of mass shootings were carried out by people who played violent video games.

Staying
OPEN-MINDED

The debate about violence in video games shows no signs of ending anytime soon. Different studies and the opinions of different groups of scientists are used by people on each side of the debate.

As new studies are done and new facts are found, a person's point of view can change over time. It's good to be open-minded about important issues. It's also natural to change your opinion as you grow and learn new things. Your opinion of violent video games in the future may not be what it is today, and that's okay!

Know the Facts!

A 2015 study showed that 82 percent of teenagers said they feel happy when playing video games, and 30 percent said they feel angry.

Are **video games** too **violent?**

YES

- Some video games are so violent only adults can play them.

- There's a link between video games and aggression.

- Violent video games can lead to a lack of empathy.

- Video games can cause people to become desensitized to violence.

- Some people behind mass shootings played violent video games.

NO

- Ratings exist to keep kids from playing violent video games and to warn people about what's in a game.

- People can use video games to work through their aggression.

- More teenagers feel happy than angry when they're playing video games.

- Many studies on violent video games are outdated.

- Video games haven't been shown to cause violent actions.

Do you think video games are too violent? This chart can help you form your own opinion on this important issue.

GLOSSARY

aggression: Angry feelings that often show themselves as a readiness to attack.

channel: To direct feelings into a certain action.

commit: To do something—often something that is wrong.

contain: To have or include.

debate: An argument or discussion about an issue, generally between two sides.

expert: Someone who has a special skill or knowledge.

focus: Directed attention.

interact: To come together and have an effect on each other.

link: A connection. Also, to join or connect.

release: The act of making something available to the public.

violent: Relating to the use of bodily force to hurt others.

For More INFORMATION

WEBSITES

ESRB Ratings Guide

www.esrb.org/ratings/ratings_guide.aspx
The official website for the Entertainment Software Rating Board (ESRB) is a good tool for children and parents to use together to learn more about video game ratings and content descriptors.

The Video Game Revolution

www.pbs.org/kcts/videogamerevolution/index.html
This website features a timeline of video game history, quizzes about video games, and a guide to what video game ratings mean.

BOOKS

Carmichael, L.E. *How Do Video Games Work?* Minneapolis, MN: Lerner Publishing Group, Inc., 2016.

Paris, David, and Stephanie Herweck Paris. *History of Video Games.* Huntington Beach, CA: Teacher Created Materials, 2017.

Powell, Marie. *Asking Questions About Video Games.* Ann Arbor, MI: Cherry Lake Publishing, 2016.

INDEX

A

adults, 7, 8, 9, 10, 21

aggression, 12, 13, 14, 15, 16, 21

American Academy of Pediatrics, 14

American Psychological Association (APA), 14, 16, 18

C

computers, 6

content descriptors, 6, 8

D

desensitized, 18, 21

E

empathy, 18, 21

G

gaming systems, 6

I

illegal, 10

interactive elements, 8

L

laws, 10

M

Magnavox Odyssey, 6

mass shootings, 19, 21

R

rating system, 6, 7, 8, 10, 21

S

smartphones, 6

stores, 8, 10

studies, 12, 14, 16, 18, 20, 21

U

U.S. Supreme Court, 10

V

violent crime, 12